Fulfilling Prophetic Destiny

James Davis

FULFILLING PROPHETIC DESTINY. © 2014 by James Davis. All rights reserved. In accordance with the U.S. Copyright 1976, the scanning, uploading and electronic sharing of any part of this book without permission constitutes piracy and theft of the author's intellectual property. If you like permission to use the materials from this book, prior written permission must be obtained by contacting James Davis at jdavis@jamesdavisministries.com

Printed in the United States of America

ISBN-13: 978-0692327388

With honor and love, I dedicate this book to my wife, Hytholine Davis. You have always been my biggest fan. Whatever I was led to do, I could always count on your support. Thank you for believing in me. I love you very much! To my daughters, Jocelyn, Tynisha, and my son Justin, thank you for your love and faith.

Thank you…. To my father, Bishop James A Davis Sr. and my mother Doris Davis. Your support and prayers has made me who I am today. My brothers and sister, Bishop Isaiah and Dr. Gloria Williams, Apostle Levonzia and First Lady Stevens, Bishop G. Wesley and First Lady Doris Hardy, Drs. Jerry and Brenda Kelly, Bishop Harold and Dr. Brenda Ray, Drs. Marvin and Beulah Duke, Inetta Hayward, Dennis and Cyndi Houser, and Toney Black.

Introduction

Many Christians in the Body of Christ display a sense of being overpowered and frightened by the enemy, who seems to have made himself comfortable in our churches. This enemy seeks to sap the motivation and enthusiasm that Christians possessed when they first received Jesus as their personal Savior. What once thrilled us about God has now been reduced to a mere and unconvincing confession, so dry and rehearsed that demons are not threatened or intimidated when spoken to.

When we, the Body of Christ, as one decide to wholeheartedly rise up and walk out the prophetic mandate that has been placed on our lives and take our rightful place in the earth, what a powerful force we will be against the gates of hell, because we are the "Sons of God". In times past, issues and circumstances distracted us from our primary objective, but now they will be in subjection to us and our commands, because we now know and believe who and what we really are.

As you read this book I encourage you

to examine where you are in God's Kingdom. Why? Because the Master has need of you in this earth!!!

The Spirit of Average

There is a sluggish attitude in the Body of Christ that has allowed satan to infill many with a spirit of defeat. More and more we witness individuals looking for a prayer-line because they refuse to establish a *prayer-life.* A lack of perception regarding the Word of God is one of the reasons why some Christians settle for a mediocre lifestyle. The spirit of average adopts the mindset that says: "you must be like everyone else to be accepted", "God understands that the flesh is weak". "After all, you're *only* human."

However, Luke 10:19 says: *"Behold I give you power to tread (walk) upon serpents and scorpions, and over all the power of the enemy, and nothing shall by any means hurt you."* At some point we will have to accept the Word of God as being *absolute,* in order for us to be what God has anointed us to be and have what we've desired and what He promised was ours. We've all seen ourselves doing something that we have yet to actually do or having possessions that we have yet to financially acquire. And as a result of this, many have allowed their vision or hope to dissolve and eventually disappear because what was before them seemed bigger and more real than the vision or hope that was in their heart and mind.

Now, take notice of those that have moved towards their vision, *fighting the fight of faith,* taking a *"No'* and making it a *"Yes",* then seeing the manifestation of their hope and persistence. Ask them if it was easy. When you have been told *"No"* concerning things you know God placed in your heart to do it's only a set up for Him to show Himself strong and mighty through you and your faith.

So, why do we so often sit idly by while the opinions of others talk us out of our spiritual and earthly inheritance? Really, there is no justifiable reason when we have access, as we do, to the throne of God's grace. I don't know about you, but I have made a *decision of quality.* I refuse to be an embarrassment to the Kingdom of God and you should too. I refuse to be like any other preacher. I refuse to be like any other believer. As a matter of fact, I Timothy 4:12

admonishes us to, *"be an example of the believers, in word, in conversation (behavior), in charity, in spirit, in faith, in purity"*. You were not created to be like anyone else. Your destiny is unique and if you're not watchful, you will abort the plan that God has for your life.

    I encourage you to acquire people in your life that will celebrate you and not tolerate you. Introduce yourself to some new people. I'm convinced that God has *"men for you and people for your life"* (Isaiah 43:4). Years ago I heard a powerful man of God say, *"For every level you go higher, your closest friends may change"*. And I'm sure, because you're reading this book, you need some new friends. Your destiny is at stake. Your future is hanging in the balance. Don't waste time with people who are determined to mis-understand you. Set goals for your life. Learn to value your own time. If you don't, *others won't either.* Prophesy to yourself. Your own mouth is the greatest prophet you will ever meet.

Uncommon Dreamers

Uncommon Dreamers are not sidetracked by the facts, but are solely focused on fulfilling the truth about their lives. However, one of the greatest hindrances of people who dream big is a refusal to dismiss *wrong* people from their lives. Having the wrong people in your life will frustrate you. Wrong people are those who will inevitably misunderstand you. Wrong people will always pose doubtful questions and judge the validity of your dream. Their focus is on your presumed limitations and faults. They are blind to the truth that it's the wisdom and power of God that gives you the advantage. Also, wrong people may hinder the **right people** from coming into your life. You see, the right people have already noticed the company you keep and have decided, based on your choice of associates, **not to** get involved with you. If you really want to know who you are and where you are going, look at the people you attract. As they say *"birds of a feather flock together"*. Dogs run with dogs. Buzzards fly with buzzards. Eagles associate with eagles.

Uncommon Dreamers often intimidate those who have few goals. People who dream are often motivated by a higher purpose beyond where they presently are. So those who have a small vision for their lives, make an effort to assassinate the dream, character, and integrity of the dreamer. So, you see now, **uncommon dreamers attract uncommon opposition.**

But, don't be discouraged by that, because **uncommon dreamers also attract uncommon favor**. If the dream is big enough the facts don't matter. Look forward to the favor of God in your life. Job 36:11
declares, "*If they obey him (God) and serve him they shall spend their days in prosperity and their years in pleasures*". God looks forward to blessing your life. *Do you?* God does not have a problem with blessing a man both spiritually and materially when that man makes God his focus.

Regardless of the dream, expect supernatural provision to meet the need. You see God needs people that will become an open demonstration of His glory. He needs people He can put on display to demonstrate His greatness. *Why not you?* I have no problem with God being enlarged in my life – do you? If I have made Him the object of my passion, I have every right to enjoy what He has given me. Psalms 37:4 states, *"Delight thyself in the Lord; and he shall give you the desires of your heart"*. If you would get concerned about *God's dream,* I believe that you would see all of heaven manifest your dream.

Some of you reading this book already have begun to dream about your business, your ministry, your family, but when was the last time you thought about *God's business.* If you make God a priority, the money, the favor, the wisdom will be at your disposal through Holy Spirit.

Small Minds

A disastrous mistake that many make, is giving small minded people permission to create their world. Small minded people are masters at building fences. The purpose of a fence is to limit something from coming in and going out. Either way a fence is designed to create limitations. That's what small minded people do best…. *create limitations.* Mostly due to a lack of faith and personal vision for their *own* lives, they prey upon anyone who would dare to believe God. And instead of laying hold on the power of God for a supernatural lifestyle to change their own lives, they look for opportunities to kill your faith in God. Therefore they justify lack, poverty, sickness and disease as a way a Christian has to suffer. While not recognizing that Jesus nailed the curse of the law, which includes lack, poverty, sickness and disease to the cross and openly defeated hell and the grave (Colossians 2: 14, 15).

Therefore small minded people have not fully accepted what Jesus has already done, to see to it that God's people walk in daily victory. If I were you, I would qualify the people that are in my circle of friends. I would question the validity of their faith as it lines up with the Word of God. As I have previously stated, you're the biggest prophet that you would ever meet. Because what you think and say about yourself can make void the opinions of your enemy or strengthen every negative confession they have made about you.

Serve notice to the fence-builders! **Let them know that you're breaking out! It's your time to go over the wall!** Don't let another day of the opinions of others be a prison cell for you. **It's your time** to receive the favor, success and goodness of God in your life! God's word is truth. If you become parallel with the Word of God, there is nothing that will be denied that God declares is already yours. Jesus went to the cross for your future. God's will is for you and I to receive everything that we need to restore us back to our place of dominion (Genesis 1:26).

God's Will

From a legal standpoint, a last will of testament cannot be executed until the one that has legal authority over the contents of the will passes away. Then and only then, is the desire of the one who died, carried out among those who should be the recipients of the will. Well, Jesus had a will that all mankind would be restored back to his original relationship with the Father. However, in order to accomplish this, it had to be at the expense of His life. But, unlike in the natural, when one dies the will may get held up from being executed because of the infighting that may go on between the parties who are the recipients of the will. Jesus arose from the grave to assure that everything you and I are supposed to receive from His will would not be held up or denied. Therefore, you and I are without excuse. The day has come for the children of God to lay hold on the provisions of His promises. I suggest you *stop making excuses and start making the adjustment.* No one is holding you back. No one can limit you concerning the things of God except you. *Stop complaining about what you permit.* Your destiny is in your hands and in your mouth. Start believing that with God **all things are possible.** (Luke 1:38).

The Tabernacle

I relate the destiny of the believer to the Old Testament Tabernacle. All three areas of the Tabernacle represent progression in the life of one who is moving in alignment with God's divine purpose for their life. Three various stages of progression are associated with the Tabernacle.

The first stage in this worship experience associated with the Tabernacle happens in the "Outer Court". One could not proceed to go any further unless he came into contact with the Brazen Altar. The altar would force the priests to acknowledge their sins and shortcomings. You see, before we can have a true and fulfilling relationship with God, the Brazen Altar is the place where we acknowledge our need of Him.

The second stage as we continue beyond the "Outer Court" is the "Laver". The "Laver" stood midway between the altar and the tabernacle (Exodus 30:18-21). It was a round basin used by the priest to wash their hands and feet. God instructed them to wash here before entering the Tabernacle, due to the accumulation of dirt from the dry and dusty conditions of the desert. But for us, it denotes a command from God to exhibit a holy life, separating us from the dirt and filth of this world's system. To fulfill the prophetic mandate on your life, you cannot allow yourself to become polluted and contaminated by the desires of your flesh and the ungodly influences of your surroundings. So while the "Laver" experience is necessary, it alone is not adequate.

You see, what takes place in the Outer Court is just that, an experience that happens outside. No covering is provided in the Outer Court. That's why God demands covering. **Covering denotes accountability and fellowship.** The Father has given us the covering that we need, in that of the governmental gift of the Pastor and the local church. Your Pastor's assignment is to not only feed you spiritually, but also to provide a haven where your gifts and callings can be developed.

Friend, if you believe God wants to move you to the next level and next dimension of your life, you must allow your life and ministry to be covered by *something and someone* bigger than you. Even if you are a Pastor, reading this book, you also need a Pastor. I believe what has helped me get through overwhelming situations in ministry is the fact that I am connected to something bigger than me. You see, it's no need of reinventing the wheel, when it already exists. Elevation and promotion in the Kingdom of God is determined by your connection to spiritual covering. Gone are the days of the "Lone Ranger".

The Lone Ranger is the individual who has a calling of God upon their life, but they attempt to fulfill this calling by themselves and with their own perception of fulfillment. They don't understand that we are all connected in the building of the people of God (Ephesians 4:11). Lone Rangers resist the opportunity to seek counsel. Why? Usually it's because of pride. You see, pride tells an individual not to ask questions, because it will reveal to others that you are unsure of your assignment. Therefore they *"compare themselves among themselves"*

(2 Corinthians 10:12).

Also people with the "Lone Ranger" syndrome have a tendency to fight and resist the task of being accountable to someone else, mainly because of the insecurities they feel. When the term "accountable" occurs in a conversation, some are inclined to become very suspicious. But you must understand that accountability and fellowship provides an atmosphere where wisdom and strength can be transferred. You're only as sharp as the people you are accountable to and in fellowship with. Proverbs 27:17 declares that *"Iron sharpens iron"*. This iron also sharpens your character. You see, it is not your charisma (gift) alone that God is requiring, but your character as well. Your character will take you into places where your gift can't keep you. If you master and spend time developing your character as you would your gift, then you have proven to God that you can be trusted to represent Him anywhere. I encourage you to unite with the vision of your Pastor and your church fellowship. Why? The prophetic word is always attached to something bigger than you. Allow God to birth in you His predestinated plan for your life and stop living without spiritual covering.

The Inner Court

The "Inner Court" is where revelation and understanding of who you really are begins to unfold. It's in this time of your life that the three pieces of furniture that were located in the Inner Court provide a glimpse of what God has said about us and how our intimate relationship with Him is to develop. The furniture included: the Table of Showbread, Candlesticks and the Altar of Incense.

Let's explore three important facts about the Table of Showbread. First, because of their nomadic lifestyle, the children of Israel needed furniture that was strong and durable for frequent transports. The Table of Showbread was made out of acacia wood. This wood was considered to be very durable, located in the desert. Its strength and resilience allowed it to survive the hot desert climate. So it is with you, your destiny will require you to survive the harshest of opposition and environments. Your enemies will use whatever they can to distract you from your purpose, through false accusations, harsh and unjustified criticism. Someone told me that false accusation is the last step just before a promotion. *So go ahead and rejoice!!* **Because what your enemies don't know is that you're about to be promoted!**

Secondly, Jesus who is our living bread sustains us while we bring resolve to key areas of our lives. You are what you eat. And if the Word of God is what you have been nourishing yourself with, then you can expect to become and have what the Word of God says is yours.

Thirdly, a table with food placed on it speaks of fellowship. No one in the Kingdom of God can advance without fellowship. Jesus declared that *"where two or three are gathered together in my name there am I in the midst"* (Matt18:20). Our Father promotes fellowship, because fellowship promotes accountability. You can't be around Kingdom minded people consistently and continue to hide your weakness. Fellowship exposes the vulnerable places in our lives and forces us to confront our shortcomings.

The Candlestick typifies Christ as our light. It is noteworthy that natural light was shut out of the Inner Court. Therefore, any light seen in the Inner Court radiated from the Candlestick. So as it was with the Tabernacle, so it is with us. The Word of God illuminates our purpose. The inability to see the plan of God for our lives is a result of us being blind to our true purpose. Far too often, many in the Body of Christ go through the cyclical effects of blindness. As we draw nearer to God, we constantly see and are thrilled about our purpose. However the moment we back off of continued revelation, we stagger and grope around as one that is blind and spend vast amounts of time sidetracked and distracted from God's intention for our life.

The Altar of Incense is where we find rest from the negative opposition that has confronted us. The focus of this altar positioned the priest for praise and worship. This is where we as believers began to understand why we were rejected. Why we didn't fit in. Why we were falsely accused.

Our true purpose and identity starts to make sense to us.

It is sometimes through adversity that we really come full circle with our anointing and began to understand that challenges can be a good thing. It is in this season that the believer stops moaning and whining and begins to rise to the mandate that is on their lives and all the *Whys* are finally answered. Past prophetic directives and instructions are given a reason for their existence. All of a sudden the prophetic word becomes a reality. And because we began to understand the opposition that has attacked our lives, our worship takes on new meaning. Our focus is off of the challenge and we began to be glad and thankful because everything that was intended to destroy us actually promoted us. It is because of this new found revelation that we are now ready to enter the Holy of Holies.

Holy of Holies

In the Holy of Holies, like the Old Testament priest you are so consumed by the Glory of God that is now overflowing out of your life, there is nothing that your enemies can do to stop what God has begun. This level of glory validates the price you had to pay to become who you are. People who used to easily upset you, no longer have your focus or attention. And you have even forgiven them! You are so consumed by your new assignment that you become unstoppable. This new outlook on your destiny has all of a sudden shaken up your old identity. You have been propelled from the *"shall be" of the Word, to the "now of the Word!!*

It becomes vitally important that now you began to guard your heart concerning the purposes and plans of the Father for your life. New friends are now a key component of your future. People and things that don't promote growth in your life must be given their *eviction notice.*

Because, if they are allowed to remain attached to you in any shape or form they will choke the prophetic word of God over your life and you will began a digressive movement away from your future. The Apostle Paul makes an explosive declaration about his own life in Philippians 3:13 "this one thing that I do, **forgetting** those things which are behind and reaching forth to those things which are before".

Pressure

It is because of who we are in Christ that your enemy will attempt to create insurmountable pressure in your life in order to get you to renege on the prophetic Word of God over your life. It is at this level of your anointing that you must be in control of your emotions so that when pressure hits, you will rehearse what God said. I'm convinced that one of the greatest deliverances that you can ever have, is to be delivered from emotions that are out of control. <u>Never make a permanent decision while in a temporary situation.</u> Too many believers have and are continuing to fall short of the provisions of God because they refuse to arrest their emotions and bring them under the subjection of Holy Spirit. You can move easily out of the will of God in any area if your decisions are emotionally based and not grounded on the Word of God.

    That's why your life must reflect Matt 12:35 *"A good man out of the good treasure of the heart brings forth good things: and an evil man out of the evil treasure brings forth evil things"*. What comes out of you is what's been *living* in you! The reason why believers can make a bad confession with their mouths is because of the negative thoughts that are harbored in their hearts. You can't really live beyond your heart-life. If we are going to reflect what God has said then our diet must consist of the Word of God. It becomes imperative that we understand that our future is depending on what we are decreeing now. You can expect your purpose and future to become fulfilled at the level you allow Holy Spirit to illuminate your mind in all that God has declared is possible. It is the fault of the believer who refuses to transform their mind and allows the sewage of familiarity to pollute the pool of their destiny.

I'm reminded of Mark 6:1-5 how Jesus' ministry was hindered in Nazareth because of the failure of those around Him to move beyond the familiarity of Jesus' past in order to see His present day assignment. As a matter of fact, verse 5 says *"And he could do no miracle there"* NAS. Even though Jesus was in the midst, faith wasn't present, so even the ministry of Jesus was hindered. Not because He wasn't anointed, but man's inability to believe.

I believe that all too often some of the most gifted and anointed people you could ever meet in life have allowed their past and their present predicaments nullify the power of God in their lives. Because they have failed to embrace the leading of Holy Spirit, they have succumbed to whatever pressure their present situation offers.

I'm declaring unto you that you are not to let another day go by that satan is permitted to take advantage of you. The *possibilities* of God rest in you. *With God all things are possible.* Don't throw away this moment. The Father has invested Himself in you. Make the dividends count.

Understanding Your Moment

Ecclesiastes 3:1 declares *"To everything there is a season and a time to every purpose under the heaven"*. There comes a time in every believer's life that they must sense when it is their moment. If you are really in tuned to Holy Spirit you can discern when the *winds* in your life are changing. It is through this process that our character is be reviewed by the teacher of all teachers (Holy Spirit). I'm inclined to believe that most of us want God's will and favor to be demonstrated in our lives. It's the process of development that is despised. However it is through this training and mentoring that the best of us is brought forth.

Jeremiah 18:1-6, gives us a glimpse of a potter and the development that is involved to bring out the best that the clay has to offer. *"O house of Israel cannot I do with you as this potter? says the Lord. Behold, as the clay is in the potter's hand, so are ye in my hand."* You must not fight against the development.

You see, growth is a natural process. But development is a result of continuous exercise. For example, in the human body we all have the same muscles, however there is reason the body-builder's muscle are more defined and clearly visible. That person takes the time to add pressure to their muscles through weights. Over a period of time and constant pressure being applied, that muscle begins to protrude through the skin and its size and shape allows the body to do what an underdeveloped muscle can't do.

And so it is with your character. Through submission to Holy Spirit you will be enrolled in a journey with God that will fashion His personality and likeness in your life. You become like Him in character, wisdom and anointing. You begin to expect the power of God to be so strong in your life that whatever He instructs you to do; you are ready to do it. The threats and barks of your enemies are now so insignificant, because you have been in the presence of God.

I sense because you're reading this book you don't want your moment to come and you were not ready to take advantage of it. Too many dreams and ideas have been swept up on the shores of *bad timing*, because the dreamer didn't realize when it was or was not their moment. And because they could not discern their opportunity they missed their moment. When we miss the "moment" that God has given us we have a tendency to launch out of season. And because the dream is out of season, it fails to produce what was in the heart of the visionary. Therefore, the blame is made against the dream, however, the problem is not the dream but in the timing.

Faith

Hebrew 11:1 states "Now faith is....." I believe the first three words of this scripture is key to understanding the entire chapter. So it was with the saints of old, so it has become with us. We must recognize that God has given us faith for the "now". That faith is a present help. As citizens of the Kingdom of God, our fight is not with the devil, but our ability to receive the finished work of Jesus. As our salvation began by faith (Romans 3:27- 28), the life we are called to live must be demonstrated *in* faith.

For the believer, the "Law of Faith" (Romans 3:27) has to be a foundation to their life if he or she is to fulfill their prophetic destiny. The believer must govern their lives by this, because it is what pleases God (Hebrews 11:6). It was by this very principle that He created all things. Our Father spoke it and it became. So you see the creative power that rest in our Father was also in the life of Jesus. If it was in the life of Jesus, then it must also be in our lives. This why in Mark 10:27 we are told *"With men it is impossible, but not with God"* We must make the transformation in our mindset from just being "mankind" to becoming "God-kind".

Conversion vs. Conviction

Conversion points to a change in mind, a change of a mental position. But in most cases it is only temporary. Furthermore when the flesh is under pressure the decision to please God will not prevail because the individual had a conversion, *but not a conviction.* There are many who know what to do to please God, but they don't follow through with the behavior to carry it out. The missing element is a conviction.

A conviction is an established standard that does not only rest in the mind, but it is an immutable law that rest in the heart. Regardless of the circumstances, this person has decided that they will not displease God and will not allow others to encourage them to do so either. You see, you cannot change your theology to accommodate your situation. What delivers you from a circumstance is your conviction of the Word of God to get you through and over any situation. You cannot allow your integrity to be compromised and your testimony to be corrupted because you are in a "storm". It is your conviction of the fact, that the Father loves you and according to Isaiah 54:17 no weapon, no persons, no lies….will prosper against you! Your conviction allows you to hold your course, knowing that God's word will promote you if you stay committed to your conviction. It was Joseph's conviction of displeasing God that gave him the strength to push back the sexual advances of Potiphar's wife (Genesis 39:9). This was no doubt sexual harassment in the workplace. And even though he could have taken advantage of her many advances, he had a revelation and a conviction of God that strengthened him under the pressure.

I challenge you to take back your conviction of righteousness. Your conviction will establish the boundaries around your life and hold your integrity intact. You don't have to compromise your conviction for "people pleasing performances". If you are not convicted of what God says you are, people will manipulate you into becoming what they think you should be and will drain your anointing to fulfill carnal opportunities.

Kingdom Language

Matthew 12:34-35 declares *"Out of the abundance of the heart the mouth speaks."* It also emphasizes that the climate of your heart will determine the quality of your words. According to Webster's dictionary, the definition of quality is the degree of excellence in which a thing possesses. Your words are your life. Your words have the ability to *increase* you or *decrease* you. The Kingdom of God will require you to evaluate the quality of your vocabulary. As believers it is imperative that your words do not become a snare (trap) to your soul (Proverbs 18:7). Your level of articulating your environment cannot be on the same level as of the world system. The revelation of your destiny and circumstances has to exceed those who are not aware of what the Word of God says.

This Kingdom mandates that you cannot use your mouth to bless and curse (James 3:10). What do you mean by curse? I'm saying that anytime God has given you His word in a matter and you speak contrary to the "word" concerning that situation or person, you just cursed. Webster's dictionary states that to curse, you have spoken evil or has caused injury with your mouth.

This is what happened in Numbers 13:32. All twelve spies agreed that the land was plentiful and full of abundance.

However, ten of those spies **cursed** the promise through a testimony of unbelief, which in turn caused the congregation to lose hope. You can speak ill of God's promises to the degree that they become ineffective in your life. Because, you struggle to believe a promise of God, you can also influence others to struggle as well. In other words *the Word of God will still work,* but it won't work for you and others because of unbelief.

To Be or Not To Be

Romans 12:2 challenges us to *"prove what is good and acceptable and the perfect will of God"*. It is not enough for you to be saved from your sins, but you must become the living proof of a Kingdom citizen. Therefore you must represent Christ and represent Him well. You either are or are not a Kingdom citizen. There are no grounds for neutrality. Far too often many Christians just want to be "rapture ready" but when it comes to being the "proof" of their faith, they easily play the "victim of their circumstances". This in turn creates a path that diverts them from the responsibility of having to take a stand against the gates of hell. I John 5:4 states, *"Whatever is born of God overcomes the world. <u>And this is the victory</u> that has overcome the world – our faith"*.

Romans 8:19 says that *"creation is waiting for the manifestation of the sons of God"*. It's imperative that the believer stand in their rightful place, so that the world has something to hope in. We who have taken on the character and nature of Christ are required to be the proof of who we say we are. Drown yourself in His likeness. Let's show the world what Kingdom citizens look and act like. Let's give them a reason to want a righteous lifestyle.

Overcoming a Setback

No one in the Body of Christ is exempt from a setback. There is no one who has done anything that has not tasted the pain of a mistake. *But, there is good news!* For truly if you have learned from the mistake, you are still a success in the making. Why? Because you've learned what <u>not</u> to do.

Now once we get the Wisdom of God in our particular circumstance, we can expect to recover from whatever dilemma we were in. Micah 7:7 declares *"that we will look to the Lord…..our God will hear us."* I want you to know that the God we serve is able to bring us back from a setback. I have certainly experienced my share, and some of those times my enemies took comfort in seeing me in tough situation. But guess what, I did not stay in the tough times. As a matter of fact Micah says in chapter 7, verse 8 "Do not rejoice over me my enemy; when I fall, I will arise! Glory to God! I know what it's like to minister the Word of God and yet no money is in the bank account, car repossessed, lights disconnected at home, no groceries in the refrigerator, must I go on? Why am I sharing this, you ask? Because I want you to understand that I know what a setback is and what it can do to your self-esteem. The devil will play on your mind and tell you that you are not a Christian, because Christians don't have those kinds of problems. Also your problems are a further indication that God is not with you. What will your family say? Your friends? People in your church? So in the midst of a setback, we must refocus ourselves on God who is full of compassion and favor towards us. It is His unfailing love for us that causes us to recover from any calamity. *"His strength is made perfect in our weakness"* (2 Corinthians 12:9). I say to you, hold your head up! Square your shoulders! Look the devil in the eye and remind him *"Greater is He that is in you than he that is in the world"* (1John4:4). Keep in mind **a set- back is a step-back for an opportunity to make a comeback!**

The Process and the Product

Webster's dictionary defines the term "process" as "the course of development" Everywhere you look, furniture, automobiles, glass, metals, even people experience process. The walk of the believer requires a day to day presence with the Father. Only in His presence are we being refined to look and act just like Him. Jeremiah 18:1-6 shows us that God desires to shape and fashion us into an image that reflects Him. This "process" of reflection can be painful and yet rewarding. You see, the Father loves you and me so much that He desires for us to experience His glory daily. In order to get us to that place there has to be a character make-over. This character make-over may require you to release some things that you would rather hold on to. I am amazed at the testimony of people who say they want to be everything that God wants them to be. But, in reality they really want to be used on their own terms and established conditions. In other words, conforming to the image of Christ and His assignment on their lives has to be by their own standard.

Perhaps in my observation, we have been spoiled, because others have made excuses for us so long and have justified the laziness in the Body of Christ that we've observed. But thanks be unto God, that He still has a remnant of people who are not conforming to the religious church, but to the Kingdom of God. This group of believers has decided that the glory of God is going to be seen on them and in them so devils will back up and recognize that they have been with Jesus. Will you be part of that group? Can you be counted on to make a Kingdom difference? Or will you continue on with church as usual; still making excuses for your shortcomings?

Kingdom Givers

You see anybody can be a church member. However, there is a shortage of members who really care about the vision of their Pastor and the local church. As a matter of fact they never even ask about the vision or what could they do to help bring it to pass. They are simply satisfied with minimal church attendance; they sparsely give their tithes and sow seeds into the local church. When asked to give anything extra they whine about what they don't have. Whether it is the Pastor's Anniversary or Birthday they continue to make excuses as to why they can't give. Never mind the fact that these celebrations come the same time every year. When it's time for a mission trip or an opportunity to bless others, for some reason it's never a good time for them. But Kingdom givers are those who are continually looking for opportunities to be a blessing. They have a heart for the ministry's vision and are willing to do their part to bring about the fruition of the vision. They recognize it's not always what they give but also in the attitude of how they give. Did you notice the Bible says that God loves a cheerful giver, not the *biggest giver*? That is not to excuse a person who gives large. Keep in mind, your harvest is based also on your attitude and not on the amount alone. So, Kingdom believers know that whatever they do or give in the local church accompanied by a willing and sincere attitude their gift goes further and the harvest of their gift is greater.

2 Corinthians 9:8 states that *"God is able to make every earthly favor and blessing come to you in abundance, so that you may always and under all circumstances and whatever the need be self- sufficient"* (Amp.). This is a powerful scripture for the believer to grab a hold of. However it cannot sit alone without verses 6 & 7.

You see, the favor and earthly blessing comes in proportion to an individual's giving to the Kingdom of God. If you notice verse 6 of that same chapter shares two dynamics. That is, he who gives little also reaps or receives little. And he, who gives much, receives much. In addition, verse 7 points out the attitude in giving. Therefore the blessing of verse 8 is contingent on verses 6 and 7. I can tell you from personal experience that giving to the Kingdom of God can spur the pace of your purpose and destiny. You see, for everything I have, I made it my purpose to sow for it. I remember when my family and I believed God for a home. I was sitting in my living room listening to a preacher who believed God for a home. Holy Spirit immediately told me that I needed to give. So, I obeyed what Holy Spirit told me to do and in a few days I was approved for a beautiful 4 bedroom, 2 ½ bath home.

    Let's look at another example, Philippians chapter 4. All across the Body of Christ we all are familiar with verse 19 in which the Apostle Paul states that *"God will supply your every need according to His riches in glory in Christ Jesus"*. What a wonderful promise! But this scripture many have missed. When you look at this scripture in the context that it is written, Paul is writing to the church at Philippi. He is reminding them of their continuous financial support to his ministry. He states in verse 15 that no church partnered with him in ministry but them. He further states in verse 16, that this was not just a one-time seed. But they performed this act "once and again."

I believe this is a good place to emphasize this. When a farmer is looking for a harvest, he just doesn't plant a seed one time and in one spot. He recognizes that if he is going to harvest a whole field of crops that he needs to sow seed(s) in the entire field. Therefore he is not going to sow one- time or in one section. My brothers & sisters you must understand the entire Kingdom rides on the principal of Seed-time & Harvest (Genesis 8:22). It's your continuous giving that ushers in the harvest.

It was the continuous giving of the church at Philippi that allowed Paul to prophetically state that their giving was abounding to their Kingdom account (verse 17). Verse 19 is an announcement of the benefits that was upon this small church because they financially supported his ministry. So in other words the prerequisite to manifesting verse 19 is to fulfill verses 15 and 16.

Proverbs 11:24-25 encourages us to sow seeds. Remember your seed may not just be money, but be *anything* that you expect a harvest from. Therefore don't sow what you don't want to reap. Keep this in mind everything you do towards one another is a seed. Showing mercy, kindness, compassion, loves, giving to charity, speaking a kind word, etc. are all liberal acts of giving that shall increase the giver.

While I'm on the subject of giving and receiving I might as well as discuss the supporting of ministry gifts in the Body of Christ. We live in a world where God has given men and women many things to improve their lives. And these things are not just for the "world" to enjoy but they also belong to the people of God's Kingdom. It grieves me to see people mentally and verbally approving the CEO of a major corporation, a professional athlete, or a major Hollywood celebrity having the finer things in life, but the local church pastor is supposed to only have enough to sustain him or her. In some church circles it is still expected for the pastor or priest to take a "vow of poverty". No CEO or Hollywood celebrity speaks life into your life like your local Pastor does or any other ministry gift (Ephesians 4:11). If anyone should enjoy life and what it offers, it is a man or woman who has sold their soul to the Gospel of Jesus Christ. Paul points out in 1 Corinthians chapter 9, because he has sown spiritual things into the lives of the church he has a right to receive material things. Deuteronomy 25:4 states that you don't *"muzzle an ox that treads out the corn"*. In other words don't withhold the opportunity from the individual who is feeding you, the opportunity for them to eat as well. When the pastor of a local church is allowed to flourish and do well the whole church reaps the benefits. If a man or woman who is feeding you the Gospel of Jesus Christ and it's changing your life for the better, you should be a blessing to them in a tangible way. Your Pastor's birthday or ministry anniversary should never be overlooked. If it is, it simply means that you don't really appreciate the gift in the form of your Pastor that you have.

You see, fulfilling your prophetic destiny is determined also in how you take care of those you have been entrusted in the growth of your spiritual development especially your Pastor who is the overseer of the local church. Their responsibility is to build and equip you for your life's assignment. Therefore when you take care of them, you are also investing in yourself. Any church that intentionally neglects to support their Pastor and ministry gifts financially has simply not read the Bible in this area and will not prosper.

The Law of the Lid

There is a leadership principle in the business community called the "Law of the Lid". In this principle a demonstration is done with a flea. Once this flea was caught it was placed in a jar with a screw on lid. For several minutes this flea would attempt to jump its way out of the jar, but unfortunately it kept hitting the lid. After several attempts a "conditioning" sets in. In other words this flea begins to become conditioned to the fact that there is a barrier that is keeping him from leaving the confines of that jar. At some point the flea stops attempting to escape the jar and. If you are a leader over a group of people, recognize that as a leader you must continue to develop and grow so that those under you will have space to move forward. In other words, <u>don't become the lid.</u> It's dangerous for a leader to stop growing and developing. Because stagnation and complacency can creep into an organization and soon new ideas will cease to flow. This is how tradition is allowed to flourish in any organization, because the effectiveness of our assignment is no longer being pursued. Therefore, that leader will continue to work with outdated methods and programs that are inferior and non-productive.

    For the person working under the leader, it's imperative that you not only encourage your leader, but look for opportunities to assist them in growing. Keep in mind that your own elevation cannot go higher than the lid. So your future growth is connected to your leader. Jesus stated that the servant is not greater than the teacher. Therefore God is not going to circumvent a leader to promote a follower. Luke 16:12 states *"And if you have not been faithful in that which is another man's, who shall give you that which is your own".*

Addicted to Chaos

There are some people that I believe that are addicted to chaos and drama. Their life is one soap-opera story after another. They haven't been at peace with themselves or others for so long that if they got a moment of calm they would think something was wrong or someone is out to get them. These people are spiritually schizophrenic. Picking a fight is their way of having the last say so in a matter. This individual will never fulfill their destiny, because they must understand that we never become pleasing and fulfilling to God by hurting other people. Remember, *hurt people only hurt people.*

Recognizing Your Assets

I often say that a person's greatest asset is not what he has in the bank only, but in the relationships they have. You see the time will come in all of our lives that certain situations cannot be rectified with money or lavish gifts. God is going to use someone to favor you. Like Joseph in the Bible, it took someone else to promote him as a ruler in Egypt. Even though he had the anointing of wisdom upon his life, God used someone else to promote him.

In Genesis 39:3 it states that Joseph's master saw that the Lord was with him and verse 4 states" Then he made him overseer or as we say in our modern day vernacular "supervisor". While being thrown in prison due to the false accusation of attempted rape, he was made the "head prisoner" by the jailer. (Genesis 39:22). Eventually his ability to discern dreams brought him before Pharaoh who made him a ruler in Egypt (Genesis 41: 40). Even though he had the favor and anointing of God upon his life, he could not fulfill the destiny of his life without being promoted by someone else. Joseph's gift got him before the people who could take him further than he was able to get on his own (Proverbs 18:16).

In Genesis 40, we see how Joseph met Pharaoh's butler while in prison. Isn't it funny how God *will allow* you to meet people through situations you thought you would never be in. Places you would have never chosen, opportunities you would have walked away from, and people who you would have never chosen to be with, yet you ended there because of a divine purpose. Wow! *That will preach all by itself!*

But getting back to Joseph, while in prison he interprets the dream of the butler and then is forgotten about. Two years later, Pharaoh has a dream that nobody could interpret. All of a sudden his butler remembers Joseph and tells Pharaoh about him. You know the rest of the story. Joseph is promoted and put in charge of Egypt's economy during a famine.

My point is that while we often hear

preached that Pharaoh promoted Joseph; we forget that the difference between the prison and Pharaoh's palace was *the butler*. In other words you don't need *everybody* to like you, just the *right person* to like you. It was through one man, that Joseph's life took a different course. Instead of trying to be liked by everyone, look for favor from the one person that is the difference between your prison and the palace. Most of the people you are trying to please will never do anything for you anyway. When was the last time any of your friends called just to say they felt *led* to pay your mortgage, rent, or car payment? My point is, that one person can make the difference between your today and tomorrow, *just one*.

If you take notice of this story you should also recognize that God used a pagan government (Pharaoh) to promote Joseph. This simply means that when our heavenly Father has a plan for you, He will use anything and anyone to get you to your destiny. Don't attempt to pick and choose your course, because you are more than likely going to choose the wrong route and the wrong people to get you there. You must discern and listen to Holy Spirit when choosing the people to help you in the fulfillment of your destiny. Your best friends don't always qualify. Sometimes it's not even your church friends that God is going to use to bless you. The person or persons for your life may be across town or across the country.

Geographical Shift

Because of your assignment, you may be forced to leave the comforts of your surroundings. This shift doesn't always mean leaving your city or church, it could also mean your present neighborhood or employer. Genesis 12 allows us to see a man named Abram. His family worshiped many gods. But our God (Yahweh) "I AM" wanted to do something new and establish a covenant with Abram. However the requirement of this new relationship required a geographical shift. Even though the Bible does not mention it, I'm led to believe this move may not have been a move of comfort for Abram, because he was well up in age to move and up root his family. But verse 4 of chapter 12 says *"So he departed as the Lord had spoken to him".*

This passage of scripture is very personal to me, because I too had to make a geographical move. Sometimes what the Lord has placed in your life, your surroundings may not be conducive to the gifting in your life. There are times that the Lord will lead you into a place of unfamiliar territory. And the purpose of this new place is to draw out of you something that will flourish and be a blessing to your life and to others. One of the things that I appreciated while making a geographical move was the will to explore "new territory" It became a catalyst for the increase of my faith. You see, in "new territory" you don't always have the influence of others to get you in and out of certain situations. You simply have to trust God completely.

My personal experience in moving from Richmond, Virginia to Virginia Beach, Virginia afforded me the opportunity to see if what God had told me was really true. Even though my move was not very far, the new location offered something different for my ministry and business acumen. As we say in the business community: location, location, location! You will find that certain climates, geographical boundaries, landmarks, business communities, financial districts, etc. all of these categories have an effect on the type of people that live in those areas. The mindset of people are shaped and developed simply because of where they live and what resources are available.

Therefore you must determine not only what is your assignment but to whom you are assigned to and what area or community will allow you to maximize your gifting, abilities and talents.

This move should not be done without prayer and counsel from someone who is mature in the things of God and has your best and not their best interest at heart. You see the Bible says in the "multitude of counsel there is safety". That's why pastoral covering is essential. A true man or woman of God will not attempt to stop you but they will be open to prayer and offer you Godly counsel. You also should consider fasting during this time of change so that Holy Spirit can reveal to you the pros and cons of this transition. Hearing the voice of God is essential to your faith and confidence that this is what the Lord will have you to do. You want to be right in the will of God concerning this. Holy Spirit takes all of the guesswork out of this move. This is why it can't be a sudden shift.

As a Pastor I get leery of people that all of a sudden have to move. Especially when they have responsibilities and have not notified and prepared others concerning their departure. It leads me to believe that they have a hidden agenda, have to hide or they are running from something. Because when God is involved it is orderly.

Also, be watchful of people who are not spiritual and who attempt to talk you out of a geographical shift. In many cases they mean well, however the devil will use them to get you to abort this move. Why? Because he knows the impact that you will have on the Kingdom of God and how God will use you mightily. In many cases family and friends are the last to see or recognize the power of God upon your life. They are longing to keep you around for their own reasons and not the reasons of God. However, love on them, pray for them, but keep looking to God for direction.

Lastly, **don't burn bridges!** Don't forget those who helped you to the point of where you are. Sometimes in all of our successes, we forget that our present success was made on the prayers and fasting of others. They paid the price but we reaped the rewards. I believe it is a disservice not to honor those who have been a part of our development and growth. I know that my present success is a result of others who have gone before me and are still blazing new trails. I believe that we receive a continuous flow of blessing from the Lord because we choose to honor our fathers and mothers both naturally and spiritually. You will never know who you will need in life and burned bridges cannot be rebuilt in a day. As I stated before, relationships are of more value than money. Because the wisdom that is transferred because of the relationship will carry you and I much farther along after the money has been spent. When we honor those who have blessed our lives in the past we are also honoring God. A strict warning was given to Israel in Deuteronomy 8:10-11. They were warned that they were not to forget God after they were blessed beyond measure. And so my prayer to you is that you don't forget God or those who He used to get you into your destiny. You are to pray for them and be a blessing both spiritually and financially to them.

Planning to Win

One of the things I have discovered about people who accomplished some great things in life was that they sought a strategy to win. Sometimes this strategy was 5 years in the making, but they knew if they stuck with it, they were eventually going to accomplish what they set out to do. As a pianist, people always tell me they used to take piano lessons. But the difference in what they used to do and if they are playing now is a matter of continuation. And anything you expect to master you will have to practice and put forth the effort in order to see perfection in that area.

I believe one of the most unique words

in the English language is the word "diligence". The definition of this word means "to be consistent in effort and application". We live in a day where people give up so quickly. We give up on dreams, we give up on careers, we give up on relationships, but you must know that anything that is worth having there must be a pursuit of it. The thing you are pursuing requires a passion from you. This is why you cannot allow "hell or high water" to stop what you have seen in your mind. And I believe when God allows you to see something that is bigger than you, He didn't show it to you so you would become nervous. But he showed it to you so that you would have a hope of something better. I believe it is the will of God for the believer to want better, to live better, dress better, drive better, but most of all, please God better than they ever haved. Our Bible tells us that Christ is a mediator over *better* promises.

The Blessing

The blessing that I'm referring to here is the "Blessing" that God first pronounced upon Abraham while he was still known as Abram. This covenant in Genesis 12 was a covenant that was instituted because of God's desire to set the course for Jesus to come into the earth. God chose a man whose family were idol worshippers. I believe Abraham had the discipline already in him to obey what he believed. So all the Father had to do was turn him from worshipping idols and turn Abraham to himself (God). Therefore a generational covenant would be instituted that would reproduce a blessing on everyone that received it by faith.

This "blessing" I'm referring to positioned Abraham and his descendants to prosper and take full advantage of every situation they found themselves in. Once a man had "The Blessing" on his life there was nothing that could hold him or her down. Why? Because "The Blessing" jump-starts the favor of men and situations into a person's life. It doesn't matter how bad things are in the natural, this anointing causes them to override and have victory every negative thing in their life. You see, "The Blessing" empowers you to prosper and overcome.

We are aware of Abraham and his accomplishments because of this "empowerment to prosper". That's what "The Blessing" really is. It causes the believer to experience God's best in every situation and under all circumstances. Furthermore, this anointing to prosper was passed onto his son Isaac as well. Isaac was in a famine situation in Genesis 26. God had Isaac to stay in the city of Gerar even though the situation was not conducive for his family. Sometimes it may be while you are in a *tough* place in your life that the prophecy that was spoken over your life is ignited. It's during this time you continue to remind yourself of the "word" that has been promised to you. You keep your heart established in words that speak of your prosperity and increase. Whether it looks like it or not, you are rich just like your spiritual father Abraham (Genesis 13:2).

How Big is Your Imagination?

The word imagination gets it root from the word image. A picture, a likeness, an idea, a vision, oh I think you get what I'm saying. The problem with some people is that they have no image to pursue, therefore they are stuck in dead in jobs, dead in relationships, sometimes a dead in church, because there is an absence of an imagination. And when there is no image to follow, then there is no direction. I heard my wife, Hytholene say that "loneliness is not the absence of a companion, but an absence of direction." You have to imagine yourself not just getting by, but having more than what is needed. Don't let your present situation have you "practicing poverty". Practicing poverty is when you're constantly talking about what you don't have and what you can't do. You see when direction is clear; you become so consumed by the assignment that you don't have time to be consumed by things that are not a part of your assignment. So an imagination causes you to "see". There was a time that Abraham was absent of an imagination in Genesis 15 as to whether or not he would ever have a child. God immediately told him to look toward heaven and the stars. What God was doing was giving Abraham an image in his mind. As long as Abraham had an image of his future he could always encourage himself. He was challenged to look at the stars and if he could count them, *"so shall his seed be"* (Genesis 15:5). This is why the devil attempts to block the imagination of the believer because as long as the believer has an imagination he can "see".

The imagination is so powerful that in Genesis 11:6 the Lord says that the people under Nimrod leadership could not be restrained from anything that they imagined to do. Their imagination overrode all limitations to succeed. A person that believes in their imagination will travel across the country and the world to birth what God has shown them. Every invention and idea was birth from someone having an imagination and they pursued it. Henry

Ford imagined the automobile; Colonel Sanders, Kentucky Fried Chicken; Bill Gates, Microsoft; Ray Kroc, to improve McDonalds; Dave Thomas, Wendy's; Wilbur and Orville Wright, flying: George Washington Carver, the peanut and the list goes on. But I want to know what are you imagining? In other words what do you "see"? The possibilities of a believer is not contingent on what the devil does, *but what do you believe.* People are not your problem, your lack of a certain education is not the issue, your lack of a certain income is not what's holding you back, but your inability to take God at His word. If you want to break God's heart, let Him give you His word and you continue to doubt what He has said. Why? Because His word is His character and nature. His integrity is His word. He has nothing else to give you to change your situation, but the creative power of His word. It was His word that brought this planet into existence. And if His word can create His world, it can create yours too (Hebrews 11:3).

    The image you have of what God can do in your life is essential if you and I are going to experience supernatural results. Romans 4:18-21 allows us to see a man and woman whose physical body doesn't match up with the promise they had been given. And so like us there are times when our physical situation doesn't complement the promise from God. But, verse 18 says that Abraham hoped when he was against hope. In other words, in the natural he had nothing to look forward to. And the reason he could still have hope was because a *word* was spoken. Verse 19 states that he was not weak in faith neither did he consider the fact that physically he was incapable of producing seed.

    It's important to know that as a "faith" believer you don't put spend time meditating on the limitations but more time is spent on what's possible. Abraham chose not to spend time rehearsing what he couldn't do. Why? He had a *word.* Verse 21 states that *"he was fully persuaded that what God had promised He was able to perform".* I am convinced that as the body of Christ when we can accept what God has said; there won't be anything that we can't do that He has told us to do. There was also a key in verse 20 that I need to mention. Not only was he strong in faith, not only was he consistent in his faith, but he didn't fail to give God praise and honor.

You see that's what keeps you consistent until you see the promise come to pass. Find yourself daily with hands being lifted up and praise pouring forth from your lips. You're not praising God because of what it looks like at the moment, but you're giving Him praise and worship because of what you "see' on the horizon. You must *see it before you see it!* Find yourself giving Him praise by faith because that daughter and son will be saved, by faith that husband will come to the Lord, by faith that wife will give her life to Jesus. Don't give up on what you "see" *"Weeping may endure for the night, but joy cometh in the morning"* (Psalms 30:5b)! The situation may not be what you desire *but your praise and God's word will turn it around!*
Hallelujah!! I have had bleak situations in my own life. I know what it's like to go to bed and cry, didn't want to see the next day. But you know what? When I began to remind myself of God's faithfulness and

how He brought me out before, the tears turned into tears of joy, I began to leap and dance because I realized who I was serving and *"No weapon formed against me shall prosper"* (Isaiah 54:17). Glory to God!!!

The Fight

Do you not know there is a fight going on over the promises of God and the *Word* that has been prophesied over your life? It is a battle where in your mind the devil is attempting to get you to abort what has been said about you. The believer of today must be on guard against doubt, unbelief and false accusation. You know you are on to something when people are making ridiculous statements about you. When everywhere you turn some new rumor is being released about you. Things that have not happened, someone is reporting that it did. However take consolation in this; you must be getting ready to go somewhere or on the verge of doing something awesome because "dogs don't chase parked cars". In other words your movement is disturbing the peace of the lazy. Your sudden promotion is a reminder to those who stopped imagining, that you're about to "jump the fence". Joseph experienced that in Genesis 37:5 when he began to share his dream with his brothers. They couldn't stand the fact that he refused to be average. The only people that become enraged at others who are moving forward are those who see themselves living in a place called "stuck". This is why you choose your audience carefully. There are some things that God is revealing to you everyone in your circle of influence can't handle. You need to judge the moment you are in and learn when to release certain pieces of information about what is going on. Believe me, people who are sensitive to Holy Spirit, don't have to be told everything. They will pick it up in the Spirit and confirm to you what is happening.

This is why discernment is one of the gifts of the Spirit. This gift allows us to spiritually perceive what is taking place before us, what is happening in the Spirit and even will allow us to perceive the intentions and motivations of others.

Time

Ecclesiastes 9:11 declares that "time & chance" happens to us all. That passage of scripture highlights the fact that life offers us all kinds of opportunities. And regardless of our backgrounds, ethnicity, social order, and physical endowments, we have opportunities surrounding us. However the one thing we don't have an abundance of, is *time*.

It is the entity that we never asked for, however at birth it met us as we exited our mother's womb. The moment we took our first breath, it immediately went into operation and will not end for us until the last breath leaves our body. Now many people confuse the chances they get in life as an opportunity to regain time and that is not necessarily so. You see while a chance has resurrected itself so that you can have its moment to do what you didn't do before, the time that you had before can never be replaced but the opportunity can come again. For example if you didn't take advantage of the chance you had when you were 19 years of age to attend college, the opportunity to go to college can come again. However when you decide to go later, you just won't be 19.

However, there is one entity that does override time and that is faith. Why is this important you may ask? Because faith can accelerate time. Faith makes everything that God has promised move into the "now". What would take others months and years to obtain, faith brings a promise out of the supernatural at an accelerated rate of speed because faith is not limited by time. It's only limited by unbelief. You see the Kingdom of God is now. Not tomorrow or sometime off in the future. So as we consider the time we have and how much has been allotted to us, we are never to allow time to dictate what is possible for us. Time has only been given to us so that we are aware of where we are as it relates to the seasons of our lives.

Work

Ecclesiastes 5:19 lets us know that God who gives us riches and wealth also wants us to enjoy and rejoice in our labor. I'm convinced that the attitude that we have toward our employer can make the difference to us getting promoted, as well as opportunities to increase our skillsets.

You see God gave man work to not just support himself but also to prepare for the future. Proverbs 13:4 states that *"the soul of a lazy man always desires and has nothing"*. In other words he always wants something, but never has the means to obtain it. A person that is lazy deserves to have nothing. While reading this book if there are people in your life who are constantly pulling on you to take care of them and yet they exhibit no initiative to do anything for themselves, you tell them that I said they are lazy!!!! Get lazy people as far away from you as possible. They will drain you dry. Make sure you have not been responsible for the state they are in. Take inventory of the people you have assisted and see if they are still sitting around with their hands out.

At some point you will have to tell this person no! No doesn't mean you don't love them. It simply means that as long as you are their cushion, they will not know what it means be responsible.

The Apostle Paul states in the church to Thessalonica *"that a man that does not work should not eat"* (2 Thess.3:10). Just hearing this without understanding the context of this statement would lead one to believe that Paul seems like a very insensitive individual. Even more so how could he be a preacher making that type of statement?

The context of that statement dealt with many of the Christians in Thessalonica who were being accused of stirring up gossip and friction among each other. Also many that were part of the accused were being known as being idle and contributing little or no work at all. So Paul's statement had nothing to do with him being insensitive but to Christians who exhibited a poor work ethic.

So as it was in Paul's time, we still see the same behavior carried on today. There seems to be a mindset that God is supposed to not only supply all of our needs but will allow us to enjoy a lifestyle of abundance and favor. And you know what, it's true. As I have stated before whenever a man obeyed God, we can see from the scriptures that prosperity was one of the signs of God's approval on what he did.
A man that is committed to an assignment shall be made rich. In other words the person who is effectively minding their business (occupation) will prosper. I really believe that a person who is employed either by someone else or even self-employed attracts the assistance of God.

Did you ever notice that even in the Garden of Eden, Adam didn't just lie around and wade his feet in the river Euphrates. He was instructed to work. He had to oversee and maintain the garden. Sometimes as Christians we can become so spiritual that we don't see that through our present employment that we are being trained so that God can trust us with more. Luke 4:12 states the prerequisite to having your own business is to be committed to the business of someone else. If you would be faithful and committed where you are, you would find that opportunities for promotion and increase are waiting for you.

Let Them Go

As a pastor I've seen parents in particular drain their money, emotions and time running down behind their children who have shown no responsibility for their actions. I remember telling a mother once that as long as she continues to cushion her children's fall they will never feel the need to take responsibility. As cruel as this may sound, sometimes it is good that the child got locked up and taken off the street. Don't bail them out right away! Let them stay there so they can consider and ponder on the action that got them there. I don't know who I'm reaching with this, but stop trying to give others a quick fix. Don't get so sidetracked over one child, until you lose sight of the others who *are not* giving you trouble. Stay focused! If that person is an adult, then you must begin to do what is necessary for your own well-being.

You must understand that locked away in you is the purpose of your entire existence. But having your focus broken over situations is keeping you from your own personal growth. You see, you must keep growing, you must continue to explore new levels of *you*. You probably don't realize how exciting you are. If you don't begin to grow within, you will *die within*. And the people that have been living off of you will move on to find someone else to drain.

Passion Control

It's going to be essential you keep your passions under control. Anything that is good and yet out of control, is a train that is about to derail. When a train derails there is so much damage to clean up. The reason why a passion gets out of control is because there is no oversight and safeguards in place. In others words, **when a passion is unaccountable it will become uncontrollable.**

Let's peek into the Biblical figure of David found in 2 Samuel chapter 11. This account is like a modern day soap-opera. David is watching another man's wife take a bath. At this point in David's life those who are closets to him are gone off into battle and according to the scripture *"this was the time that kings went into battle"*. In David's case no one was around therefore his passion for this woman he saw bathing was accountable to no one. Not only did he send for the woman, but he slept with her and she became pregnant. But his passion for her did not stop there. His passion for her was so out of control that he concocted a plan to have her husband killed, so that he may have her for his own.

What we see in the life of David is not that different from today. There are people around us whose marriage is out of control; their finances are out of control, their children, their business, their church, etc. If we have areas out of control, don't make excuses. Get counseling if you must. But do whatever you have to do to get help. If you don't make the changes to take control, they will control you. For what you don't master will eventually master you. Don't become a slave to the things that are out of control in your life. Once you begin a life of covering up certain habits and behaviors you will begin a life of lies and self-destruction. Proverbs 28:13 reminds us *"that covering and making excuses for our sins will cause us not to prosper"*. And the longer you live the lie, the harder it becomes to quit. What's worse you will begin to believe your own lies. There is nothing worse than self-deception.

The moment you begin to become honest with yourself and God, you give the devil nothing to hold against you. Your sense of personal integrity becomes golden to you. You began to live at a point where you give no place to the "flesh" and give full attention to living in honesty towards others as well as with yourself.

The Presence of God

When I talk about the presence of God, I'm not talking about walking around in a room and there is a mystical fog or some halo over your head. Sometimes as Christians we are guilty of an over-active imagination. What I'm referring to as the Presence of God is an ever abiding awareness of an anointing that empowers us for day to day living.

For the businessman it may mean having the spiritual insight for engaging in contracts and negotiations. Or for the school teacher it may mean having the ability and classroom presence that quiets disruptive children. You see the Presence of God is not about making a person seem *spiritually deep* but it gives this person a commanding confidence to handle whatever situation they are facing.

The presence of God also attracts favor into this person's life simply because it acts as a magnet that draws opportunities that others may not get. And as long as this person seeks the will of God in their decision making, they will continue to experience this flow of favor.

But lets us also understand that God's presence on and in us must be "renewed" through personal time of prayer and study of the Word of God. This is where we fan the flames of our relationship with the Lord and reflect on our need of Him in our lives.

Continuing this observance will keep our relationship with the Lord fresh and exciting. Our relationship with the Lord has to be so exciting and vibrant to us, that it is noticed by others. Jesus stated that *"if he is lifted up, all men will be drawn to him"* (John 12:32). What an advertisement it could be to those who don't know the Lord, simply by the joy that is in the lives of those who call themselves Christians.

This presence of the Lord in our lives cannot be artificial. It must be real, alive and attractive to others. 2 Samuel chapter 6 records that the Ark of the Covenant which signified the Presence of God in the midst of Israel was on a cart that had stumbled. Uzziah attempted to stable the Ark by putting his hand on it. And the result was that Uzziah died right there on the spot. While Uzziah meant well, flesh was not supposed to touch the Presence of God. As it was then, it is still so now. Our heavenly Father is not interested in our man-made attempts, devices and performances that are designed to steal the focus from Him and given to men. All of our efforts to be religious without a true relationship will not last. Seek His presence, desire His glory and watch your life flourish.

Understanding Where You Are

I'm thinking of Ecclesiastes 3:1-8. This passage of scripture shows us the intervals of change that may occur in all of our lives. Solomon here states that every purpose, every intended or unintended event has a time. And I believe as we grow older and wiser we began to understand that the things that have occurred in our life were really a set-up to get us to the next level. And sometimes it took that circumstance or issue to birth the next change of events that were supposed to be. Let's peek into the early life of Moses to see what I'm talking about.

Being raised in the courts of Pharaoh afforded Moses the opportunity to experience the best of life and culture. The Egyptians with their vast understanding of complex math and language along with being known as a dominant culture of people gave Moses everything he wanted, so he thought. However with the finest of life that Moses was given, deep in his consciousness, he felt he was more. I believe that Holy Spirit was at work even at this point in Moses life. Because it was Holy Spirit that gave him his sense of consciousness and sympathy as it related to his Hebrew birthright.

Isn't it ironic how we can be exposed to certain things and even attempt to conform to what's around us and yet we know down in our spirit that God has more for us. That whatever other people are trying to get us to be, we know that their image is not what God has showed us. If I was you, I would stop trying to be who everyone else wanted you to be and move into the moment that the Father has given you. As you know Moses witnesses the harsh treatment of a Hebrew at the hands of an Egyptian taskmaster. I suppose while watching this mistreatment which was also common, there was a stirring in the heart of Moses and somehow he connected with the Hebrew being mistreated. It was this compassion that prompted him to take action and led him to take the life of the taskmaster.

Sometimes what everybody else feels is common, you are bothered by it. You see in many cases, *what angers you the most, God created you to correct.*

Well you know that this action made Moses now a traitor and his decision to escape, a fugitive. While a fugitive of Egypt, Moses wanders into the land of Midian and there meets a family that will help shape the plan and future that God had in mind for him all along. This family was not members of the local yacht club or the Chamber of Commerce. They did not have the grace and etiquette that Moses was accustomed to. Isn't it funny how the Lord can allow a situation to occur in your life where you are forced to change your place of comfort and adjust to new things? Sometime the loss of one opportunity creates another. Don't assume the losses in your life are forever. If you could see the big picture, a loss can be an opportunity to a fresh start. Stop feeling guilty about starting over. Quit trying to explain what's going on. Believe me, you will get the last laugh and all the people who snickered and laugh at your calamity, are going to apologize. If you don't believe me, ask Joseph (Genesis 45:1-15).

Moses went on to marry Zipporrah, the daughter of Jethro. And for the next forty years, Moses tended his father-law's sheep. We are looking at a man who was raised with the finest of life including food and apparel. Now it seems Moses has been reduced to living a lifestyle that is more equated with poverty and having a job assignment that would keep him filthy and dirty. But what was really happening was that Moses' was being groomed by God for the greatest task he would ever do.

As I stated before, sometimes a loss seems like life is over and the good days have come and gone. But God has a way of taking a losing situation and building things up in your life so that what you have just come through cannot be compared to what He has planned (Jeremiah 29:11). Even in Moses's new assignment tending sheep, there were some things in his character that was being defined and refined so that he would have the skill-set to lead people. The patience, discipline and leadership abilities that Moses possessed were not gained in

Egypt, but were gained while leading sheep. Moses's ministry of leading people would be accomplished by a man that God has qualified.

People will look at your life and sometimes wish they were you. They will see your accomplishments and attempt to mimic what they see but won't get the same results. If only they could hear your story, behind the story. If only they knew how many nights you may have walked the floor wrestling with God's assignment for your life and yet still believing the promise of God over your life. Sometimes there is a contradiction between what is going on in your life and what you see as the promises of God. But I encourage you to believe what God has said. It is the assignment of the enemy to get to you to doubt the integrity of God's word and believe that God has left you in a situation to die. But I've got good news for you. You're not about to die, but live! And when I say live, I'm not talking about just getting by but living an extraordinary life. Too much blood has been shed for you. Too many Christians before you have made sacrifices and given their lives so that you would be the "proof" of all that God has promised.

For some of you that are reading this book, your family and relatives still don't know who you are. I'm not talking about the childhood memories or the many mischievous deeds you may have done while growing up. But I'm talking about destiny. Mark Twain stated "there are two great days in your life; the day you were born and the day you discovered why".

Is it Your Purpose?

Many of us get so involved with all kinds of get-rich schemes and sales pitches. I too have been approached by many and a few I even got involved in. Only to discover later these opportunities were not a part of my purpose. And even while discovering this I would continue to work the business plan of the idea only to end up frustrated.

Now don't get me wrong, there are some home business opportunities that are legitimate and for the people involved in those business opportunities they are making a substantial income.

I have discovered is that for any home based business to succeed it will require consistency. With all the infomercials that you see on TV many don't notice the disclaimer that is stated at the bottom of the TV screen which reads "results may vary" or "unique testimony". In other words the creators of these businesses realize that everyone that buys into the opportunity may not all have the same financial results. So it is important that you know what you are called to be involved in.

People ask me sometimes about my opinion on certain business opportunities. Here are some questions I respond with:

1. Why this business opportunity? Is it your passion?

2. How much money do you plan to make from this opportunity? Do you have a business plan?

3. Will this opportunity draw money out of the household? And for how long?

4. Is your spouse supportive of this new

venture?

5. Whoever has asked you to join the business, have you verified how much money they have made from it?

    These are just some of the questions you need to begin to ask yourself as you consider a new business opportunity. Don't allow the questions I gave you cause you to doubt the opportunity. Just be honest with yourself. And if you do follow up with the business opportunity, give it all you have.

Understanding the Law

    One of the things, I have observed about people, especially people who have created consistent streams of income is that they have an understanding of financial laws.
    When I speak of laws I'm speaking of rules and policies that govern transactions and also are loopholes for investors and the financial savvy. Those that are determined to live an extraordinary lifestyle in most cases will pay for knowledge. For example

when was the last time you sat through a seminar of any kind involving , finances, real estate, or anything of that nature that provoked a change in how you handled the financial and investment matters in your life.

In a class I was teaching, I once asked how many people recently attended a seminar or lecture involving finances, budgeting, real estate, or any class relating to financial matters within the last year. Out of 24 adults, one hand was raised. Then I asked how many people attended a movie theatre with the last twelve months and 23 out of 24 hands went up. And then I asked the 23 people how often they attended a movie theatre and most of them stated at least twice a month, however they had not attended any type of seminar or class that was related to money with the last 12 months. In one other class I was instructing I asked the adult class about the type of books they read. And those that read books on a regular basis stated the type of books they read, including a dramas, science-fiction and fiction. However just like my previous class, no one had spent a considerable amount of time reading material that was going to have a major financial impact upon their lives.

Now I'm not saying that you should not have any other reading interest or from time to time not attend a good movie. My point is that we sometimes over indulge in activities that do not add value to our lives. Unfortunately our society is so entertainment driven, that no wonder our youth have closets with the latest fashion wear, but not doing well in school.

Those that take the time to understand the laws and rules of economics, real estate, investments, stocks and bonds, business mergers, etc. can have an advantage over the majority. And what's so bad, many of those who are acquainted and involved in the above areas that I just mentioned are hoping that others won't become knowledgeable in those areas I just mentioned. Why? Because he that has the gold, makes the rules. You see, understanding the laws and principles of a subject matter give you and I the edge to making better decisions. It also shows us how our resources can be properly used so that our resources can work for us and not us working for our resources. During the period of slavery in America, it was forbidden for blacks to be taught to read. Why? Because the oppressor knew that exposure to principles, laws and rules only gave a man a desire to be free and explore what he has read. Knowledge of one's situation and position in life would only cause the most humble slave to reject all future actions of oppression. So to keep a people oppressed, strip away their opportunities to be informed and you can forever keep an entire generation in bondage.

    It is imperative that if we're going to fulfill our destiny that information concerning financial principles and laws must be understood. I believe that God has placed these laws in the earth to show men how to take advantage of the environment, so that no one has an excuse to remain where they mentally and physically are. Once we discover our real identity in Christ, we get in motion. Along with discovering who we are we began to become a magnet that is constantly attracting information to us. Before we realize it, we are in the presence of people and opportunities that at one time in our life we could only dream about.

Stay in School

We live in a society where a person's education can open many doors for them. Furthermore, the person that desires to take advantage of every opportunity that they have been given must never cease from learning. What I'm referring to here is not just the school where you have spent a number of years learning various subjects, principles, and theorems but where you in spirit, choose to remain a student of life-long learning. What I have noticed, there is an abundant amount of people in our country who at some point were not able to attend an institute of higher learning, however that was never an excuse for them to stop learning.

Don't get me wrong, I'm not advocating that people should not place value on an institution of higher learning. But I've discovered, the paper in a frame, hanging on a wall, does not prove nor guarantee the success of that individual. It's what they have been exposed to and have applied.

You see knowledge is not power, but applied knowledge. Our ability to live an abundant and successful life is not solely determined by what stage we've walked across to receive a diploma or degree. Some of the most successful and wealthiest persons of our day did not receive the accolades of Harvard, Princeton, or Yale. However their wealth and ability to create deals and opportunities will far outnumber and run circles around the highest paid professors at any of those colleges.

The greatest business and leadership minds of our day study systems and processes. They don't waste time learning from people who have never owned a business. They don't bother with individuals who are afraid of risking it all if need be. I'm convinced that some people, who complain that they have not been given a chance at certain things in life, are only looking for a handout. Get this in your mind, no one owes you anything.

You heard the statement, feed a man a

fish and you will have to feed him tomorrow. Teach him how to fish and he'll eat for a lifetime. I'll take it a step further. Let that man get a revelation of who he is in the Kingdom of God and he'll buy the whole lake. What I don't want to see us do, is to depend on some entitlement or program to feed our dreams and ambition.

    We live in a country where there an entitlement mindset. Many who promote this are always pushing for wealth redistribution. If a person has done well in life, it's almost as if they are penalized for being successful and what they have obtained is taken and shared with others. Now don't get me wrong. I understand that there are persons who in many cases were born into environments and situations that were not their fault. In many cases, in a two-parent household they are doing all they can with two incomes and it seems they are getting further behind. So you can imagine that a single parent household may be struggling just as well. So while my response may seem insensitive, I believe that those who feel that they are at the bottom must understand that their predicament does not define who they are. I know what it is like to raise a family and not have all the funds necessary. It was in those times that I choose to take a lemon and make lemonade. Even being out of a job, wasn't going to have me "singing the blues". What I'm saying is, that if your situation is not what you want it to be then you must decide that if it is going to change it's got to start with you.

In the book of Judges, Chapter 4, there is a story of a woman who found herself in debt after her husband died. She asked the prophet what she should do. He asked her one question. *"What does she have in her house"?* In other words, what do you already possess that if it is multiplied and worked can create a better tomorrow. I can tell you from experience sometime the tools you need is already within. For example, what skills, passions and hobbies do you currently possess? It's not about getting another job on top of the job you already have. It's about recognizing that what you already possess God has given you that ability to create a better life for yourself. For Colonel Sanders it was frying chicken, which led to KFC. For Tyler Perry it was writing plays which led to the character, Madea. For Bill Gates it was programming computers which led to Microsoft.

What I have showed you, were people who had a skill and passion for what they did and when they recognized its possibilities it created for them a brighter future. Ecclesiastes 9:10-11 reminds us that "time and chance happens to us all. Let me take you back to this woman in the Bible I referred to earlier. You may be asking what happened to her. Well, the preacher she was counseling with whose name was Elijah gave her a strategy to get out of debt with what she already possessed. Because she followed and worked the plan, she not only paid off her debts. But she had enough left over for her and her children to live off of. The conclusion of all that I have just mentioned is this. Work with what you have and with what you know. Don't devalue the abilities and gifts you have to create wealth. God has no problem with you becoming wealthy. Yes I said it! Take the skills you have and decide that these skills are going to create a better tomorrow for you and your family.

Go For It!

After reading this book, I hope you will prepare yourself to maximize every opportunity that avails itself. Be prepared to bring new people in your life so that you are receiving wisdom and all available information possible. Look out for others who will attempt to get you to derail and put –off some of your plans. For people who are standing still, nothing aggravates them more than a person who is actively pursuing a goal. But it's okay because I believe after reading this book you're going to take your life to the next level.

Never mind your short comings. One of the things you will find is that you don't have to know everything. Just bring people into your life who knows what you don't know. Just master what you know.
Also give yourself space to grow and if a mistake is made, learn from it. I believe that sometimes we can be so much of a perfectionist, that we don't even take the time to relax and enjoy the process.

Take time to notice the good things in life. God has given us a wonderful world to experience. Sure problems are all around us, but make sure that the good things in life get noticed as well.

Your purpose is waiting. Go ahead and fulfill it. You're in for the ride of your life!!!!

You're only a decision away from a change….

Congratulations for completing this book. However, to really apply what you've read you must accept Jesus as your Savior and Lord of your life. If you really want to see a difference in your life, repeat this prayer of salvation:
"Lord Jesus, I want a fresh start in life. I understand you died for my sins and rose again so I can experience a good life. I surrender my will and my life to you. Thank you for accepting me. Father, I also receive by faith Holy Spirit into my life so that I am empowered to obey you. Thank you for the heavenly prayer language that you have given me as the initial evidence that I am filled with your power. Thank you for changing my life and I look forward to the rest of my life being the best of my life. In Jesus name, Amen"!!!

Praise God, Romans 10:9:10 and Acts 1:8 and 2:4 is the foundational proof that you are now saved and have a right to live an empowered life through Holy Spirit. Now I encourage you to attend and get involved in a good Bible base - Word filled church and watch your life grow by leaps and bounds. God bless you!

About the author:

James Davis attended Virginia Commonwealth University. After an encounter with God concerning his destiny, he decided to attend Bible College and received his Doctorate of Divinity from The Redeem Bible Institute. Dr. Davis, who also is a musician and singer, has dedicated his gifts unto the Lord. After serving 14 years as a Senior Pastor, Dr. Davis travels and ministers in various churches and business events. His business acumen has allowed him to have an exceptional real estate business and he uses that success to motivate others to pursue their entrepreneurial dreams and make the most of their career. With prophetic accuracy and insight along with exceptional communication skills, his goal is to convey the heart of God and help propel people to live their best life through Jesus Christ.

For speaking and bookings contact:
James Davis Ministries, Inc.,
P.O. Box 61573
Virginia Beach, Virginia 23466
www.jamesdavisministries.com
info@jamesdavisministries.com
(757) 389-2230

www.ingramcontent.com/pod-product-compliance
Lightning Source LLC
Chambersburg PA
CBHW071157090426
42736CB00012B/2362